D1231601

A Timbered Choir

Also by Wendell Berry

FICTION
The Discovery of Kentucky
Fidelity
The Memory of Old Jack
Nathan Coulter
A Place on Earth
Remembering
Two More Stories of the Port William Membership
Watch with Me
The Wild Birds
A World Lost

POETRY
The Broken Ground
Clearing
Collected Poems: 1957–1982
The Country of Marriage
Entries
Farming: A Hand Book
Findings
Openings
A Part
Sabbaths
Sayings and Doings
Traveling at Home (with prose)
The Wheel

ESSAYS
Another Turn of the Crank
A Continuous Harmony
The Gift of Good Land
Harlan Hubbard: Life and Work
The Hidden Wound
Home Economics
Recollected Essays: 1954–1980
Sex, Economy, Freedom & Community
Standing by Words
The Unforeseen Wilderness
The Unsettling of America
What Are People For?

A Timbered Choir

The Sabbath Poems 1979–1997

Wendell Berry

COUNTERPOINT

WASHINGTON, D.C.

The author thanks the editors of the following publications and pub-
lishing companies who have previously been willing to associate them-
selves with various poems reprinted here: *Amicus Journal, Beloit Poetry
Journal, The Bonfire Review, The Bread Loaf Anthology,* Calliopea Press,
*The Christian Century, Cistercian Studies Quarterly, CoEvolution
Quarterly,* Confluence Press, *Country Journal, Cutbank, Explorations,*
Golgonooza Press, *Harvard Magazine, Hudson Review, Journal of
Kentucky Studies, Kentucky Poetry Review,* Larkspur Press, *Limestone,
New England Review, Northern Lights,* North Point Press, *Ploughshares,
Poems for a Small Planet, Princeton University Library Chronicle, The
Sewanee Review, The Southern Review, Temenos, The Virginia Quarterly
Review, Wilderness.*

The story retold on page 122 (1990, VI) is from John Toland, *Battle:
The Story of the Bulge* (New American Library, 1985), 187–89.

Library of Congress Cataloging-in-Publication Data
Berry, Wendell, 1934–
    A timbered choir: the sabbath poems, 1979–1997 / Wendell Berry.
    1. Religious poetry, American. 2. Nature—Poetry.   I. Title.
PS3552.E75T55   1998
811'.54—DC21   98-4925

ISBN 1-887178-68-6 (acid-free paper)

Book design and electronic composition by David Bullen

Printed in the United States of America on acid-free paper that meets
the American National Standards Institute Z39-48 Standard.

COUNTERPOINT
P.O. Box 65793
Washington, D.C. 20035-5793

10 9 8 7 6 5 4 3

*To Kathleen Raine
and Donald Hall*

*The whole earth is at rest, and is
quiet: they break forth into singing.*

ISAIAH 14:7

CONTENTS

1985

1986

1987

1988

1989

1990

1991

1997

PREFACE

Over the past four decades, public readings of poetry have attracted a significant audience. With the obvious qualifications, I think this is a good thing. It requires us to be aware that a poem need not be just a fabric of printed words to be laboriously raveled out by students or critics, but is (or can be) written in a speakable and hearable language, the integrity of which begins and ends in the quality of its music. Public readings require us to be aware also that a poem can be a way of saying something of public interest in public: a way of making an argument, of declaring one's allegiance, of taking a stand.

This renewed public life of poetry, however, makes it necessary to say of the poems in this book that they were not conceived or written primarily as statements to be read aloud in public. I have no doubt that they can be so read; sometimes they concern themselves with issues of public importance, and I have tried always to be attentive to the way they sound when spoken aloud. What I am talking about is not necessarily a conflict. But though I am happy to think that poetry may be reclaiming its public life, I am equally happy to insist that poetry also has a private life that is more important to it and more necessary to us.

These poems were written in silence, in solitude, mainly out of doors. A reader will like them best, I think, who reads them in similar circumstances—at least in a quiet room. They would be most favorably heard if read aloud into a kind of quietness that is not afforded by any public place. I hope that some readers will read them as they were written: slowly, and with more patience than effort.

I am an amateur poet, working for the love of the work

and to my own satisfaction—which are two of the conditions of "self-employment," as I understand it. I belong to no school of poetry, but rather to my love for certain poems by other poets, some of whom, I am thankful to say, are my contemporaries.

I should say also that the poems printed here should be thought of as a series, not as a sequence. The poems are about moments when heart and mind are open and aware. Such moments, in my experience, are not sequent or consequent in the usual sense. Such a moment is not necessarily the cause or result of another such moment.

The dedication acknowledges two immeasurable debts: to Donald Hall, who has been a kind, exacting friend to these poems from the beginning; and to Kathleen Raine, whose work as poet, scholar, and editor has helped me probably more than I know.

A Timbered Choir

The Sabbath Poems 1979–1997

1979

I

I go among trees and sit still.
All my stirring becomes quiet
around me like circles on water.
My tasks lie in their places
where I left them, asleep like cattle.

Then what is afraid of me comes
and lives a while in my sight.
What it fears in me leaves me,
and the fear of me leaves it.
It sings, and I hear its song.

Then what I am afraid of comes.
I live for a while in its sight.
What I fear in it leaves it,
and the fear of it leaves me.
It sings, and I hear its song.

After days of labor,
mute in my consternations,
I hear my song at last,
and I sing it. As we sing,
the day turns, the trees move.

II

Another Sunday morning comes
And I resume the standing Sabbath
Of the woods, where the finest blooms
Of time return, and where no path

Is worn but wears its makers out
At last, and disappears in leaves
Of fallen seasons. The tracked rut
Fills and levels; here nothing grieves

In the risen season. Past life
Lives in the living. Resurrection
Is in the way each maple leaf
Commemorates its kind, by connection

Outreaching understanding. What rises
Rises into comprehension
And beyond. Even falling raises
In praise of light. What is begun

Is unfinished. And so the mind
That comes to rest among the bluebells
Comes to rest in motion, refined
By alteration. The bud swells,

Opens, makes seed, falls, is well,
Being becoming what it is:
Miracle and parable
Exceeding thought, because it is

Immeasurable; the understander
Encloses understanding, thus
Darkens the light. We can stand under
No ray that is not dimmed by us.

The mind that comes to rest is tended
In ways that it cannot intend:
Is borne, preserved, and comprehended
By what it cannot comprehend.

Your Sabbath, Lord, thus keeps us by
Your will, not ours. And it is fit
Our only choice should be to die
Into that rest, or out of it.

III

To sit and look at light-filled leaves
May let us see, or seem to see,
Far backward as through clearer eyes
To what unsighted hope believes:
The blessed conviviality
That sang Creation's seventh sunrise,

Time when the Maker's radiant sight
Made radiant every thing He saw,
And every thing He saw was filled
With perfect joy and life and light.
His perfect pleasure was sole law;
No pleasure had become self-willed.

For all His creatures were His pleasures
And their whole pleasure was to be
What He made them; they sought no gain
Or growth beyond their proper measures,
Nor longed for change or novelty.
The only new thing could be pain.

IV

The bell calls in the town
Where forebears cleared the shaded land
And brought high daylight down
To shine on field and trodden road.
I hear, but understand
Contrarily, and walk into the woods.
I leave labor and load,
Take up a different story.
I keep an inventory
Of wonders and of uncommercial goods.

I climb up through the field
That my long labor has kept clear.
Projects, plans unfulfilled
Waylay and snatch at me like briars,
For there is no rest here
Where ceaseless effort seems to be required,
Yet fails, and spirit tires
With flesh, because failure
And weariness are sure
In all that mortal wishing has inspired.

I go in pilgrimage
Across an old fenced boundary
To wildness without age
Where, in their long dominion,
The trees have been left free.
They call the soil here "Eden"—slants and steeps
Hard to stand straight up on

Even without a burden.
No more a perfect garden,
There's an immortal memory that it keeps.

I leave work's daily rule
And come here to this restful place
Where music stirs the pool
And from high stations of the air
Fall notes of wordless grace,
Strewn remnants of the primal Sabbath's hymn.
And I remember here
A tale of evil twined
With good, serpent and vine,
And innocence as evil's stratagem.

I let that go a while,
For it is hopeless to correct
By generations' toil,
And I let go my hopes and plans
That no toil can perfect.
There is no vision here but what is seen:
White bloom nothing explains
But a mute blessedness
Exceeding all distress,
The fresh light stained a hundred shades of green.

Uproar of wheel and fire
That has contained us like a cell
Opens and lets us hear
A stillness longer than all time
Where leaf and song fulfill
The passing light, pass with the light, return,

Renewed, as in a rhyme.
This is no human vision
Subject to our revision;
God's eye holds every leaf as light is worn.

Ruin is in place here:
The dead leaves rotting on the ground,
The live leaves in the air
Are gathered in a single dance
That turns them round and round.
The fox cub trots his almost pathless path
As silent as his absence.
These passings resurrect
A joy without defect,
The life that steps and sings in ways of death.

V

How many have relinquished
Breath, in grief or rage,
The victor and the vanquished
Named on the bitter page

Alike, or indifferently
Forgot—all that they did
Undone entirely.
The dust they stirred has hid

Their faces and their works,
Has settled, and lies still.
Nobody rests or shirks
Who must turn in time's mill.

They wind the turns of the mill
In house and field and town;
As grist is ground to meal
The grinders are ground down.

What stood will stand, though all be fallen,
The good return that time has stolen.
Though creatures groan in misery,
Their flesh prefigures liberty
To end travail and bring to birth
Their new perfection in new earth.
At word of that enlivening
Let the trees of the woods all sing
And every field rejoice, let praise
Rise up out of the ground like grass.
What stood, whole in every piecemeal
Thing that stood, will stand though all
Fall—field and woods and all in them
Rejoin the primal Sabbath's hymn.

VII

What if, in the high, restful sanctuary
That keeps the memory of Paradise,
We're followed by the drone of history
And greed's poisonous fumes still burn our eyes?

Disharmony recalls us to our work.
From Heavenly work of light and wind and leaf
We must turn back into the peopled dark
Of our unraveling century, the grief

Of waste, the agony of haste and noise.
It is a hard return from Sabbath rest
To lifework of the fields, yet we rejoice,
Returning, less condemned in being blessed

By vision of what human work can make:
A harmony between forest and field,
The world as it was given for love's sake,
The world by love and loving work revealed

As given to our children and our Maker.
In that healed harmony the world is used
But not destroyed, the Giver and the taker
Joined, the taker blessed, in the unabused

Gift that nurtures and protects. Then workday
And Sabbath live together in one place.
Though mortal, incomplete, that harmony
Is our one possibility of peace.

When field and woods agree, they make a
That stirs in distant memory the whole
First Sabbath's song that no largess of time
Or hope or sorrow wholly can recall.

But harmony of earth is Heaven-made,
Heaven-making, is promise and is prayer,
A little song to keep us unafraid,
An earthly music magnified in air.

VIII

I go from the woods into the cleared field:
A place no human made, a place unmade
By human greed, and to be made again.
Where centuries of leaves once built by dying
A deathless potency of light and stone
And mold of all that grew and fell, the timeless
Fell into time. The earth fled with the rain,
The growth of fifty thousand years undone
In a few careless seasons, stripped to rock
And clay—a "new land," truly, that no race
Was ever native to, but hungry mice
And sparrows and the circling hawks, dry thorns
And thistles sent by generosity
Of new beginning. No Eden, this was
A garden once, a good and perfect gift;
Its possible abundance stood in it
As it then stood. But now what it might be
Must be foreseen, darkly, through many lives—
Thousands of years to make it what it was,
Beginning now, in our few troubled days.

IX

Enclosing the field within bounds
sets it apart from the boundless
of which it was, and is, a part,
and places it within care.
The bounds of the field bind
the mind to it. A bride
adorned, the field now wears
the green·veil of a season's
abounding. Open the gate!
Open it wide, that time
and hunger may come in.

X

Whatever is foreseen in joy
Must be lived out from day to day.
Vision held open in the dark
By our ten thousand days of work.
Harvest will fill the barn; for that
The hand must ache, the face must sweat.

And yet no leaf or grain is filled
By work of ours; the field is tilled
And left to grace. That we may reap,
Great work is done while we're asleep.

When we work well, a Sabbath mood
Rests on our day, and finds it good.

XI

To long for what can be fulfilled in time
Foredooms the body to the use of light,
Light into light returning, as the stream

Of days flows downward through us into night,
And into light and life and time to come.
This is the way of death: loss of what might

Have been in what must come to be, light's sum
Lost in the having, having to forego.
The year drives on toward what it will become.

In answer to their names called long ago
The creatures all have risen and replied
Year after year, each toward the distant glow

Of its perfection in all, glorified;
Have failed. Year after year they all disperse
As the leaves fall, and not to be denied

The frost falls on the grass as by a curse.
The leaves flame, fall, and carry down their light
By a hard justice in the universe

Against all fragmentary things. Their flight
Sends them downward into the dark, unseen
Empowerment of a universal right

That brings them back to air and light again,
One grand motion, implacable, sublime.
The calling of all creatures is design.

We long for what can be fulfilled in time,
Though death is in the cost. There is a craving
As in delayed completion of a rhyme

To know what may be had by loss of having,
To see what loss of time will make of seed
In earth or womb, dark come to light, the saving

Of what was lost in what will come—repaid
In the invisible pattern that will mark
Whatever of the passing light is made.

Choosing the light in which the sun is dark,
The stars dark, and all mortal vision blind—
That puts us out of thought and out of work,

And dark by day, in heart dark, dark in mind,
Mistaking for a song our lonely cry,
We turn in wrongs of love against our kind;

The fall returns. Our deeds and days gone by
Take root, bear fruit, are carried on, in faith
Or fault, through deaths all mortal things must die,

The deaths of time and pain, and death's own death
In full-filled light and song, final Sabbath.

XII

To long for what eternity fulfills
Is to forsake the light one has, or wills
To have, and go into the dark, to wait
What light may come—no light perhaps, the dark
Insinuates. And yet the dark conceals
All possibilities: thought, word, and light,
Air, water, earth, motion, and song, the arc
Of lives through light, eyesight, hope, rest, and work—

And death, the narrow gate each one must pass
Alone, as some have gone past every guess
Into the woods by a path lost to all
Who look back, gone past light and sound of day
Into grief's wordless catalogue of loss.
As the known life is given up, birdcall
Become the only language of the way,
The leaves all shine with sudden light, and stay.

1980

I

What hard travail God does in death!
He strives in sleep, in our despair,
And all flesh shudders underneath
The nightmare of His sepulcher.

The earth shakes, grinding its deep stone;
All night the cold wind heaves and pries;
Creation strains sinew and bone
Against the dark door where He lies.

The stem bent, pent in seed, grows straight
And stands. Pain breaks in song. Surprising
The merely dead, graves fill with light
Like opened eyes. He rests in rising.

II

The eager dog lies strange and still
Who roamed the woods with me;
Then while I stood or climbed the hill
Or sat under a tree,

Awaiting what more time might say,
He thrashed in undergrowth,
Pursuing what he scared away,
Made ruckus for us both.

He's dead; I go more quiet now,
Stillness added to me
By time and sorrow, mortal law,
By loss of company

That his new absence has made new.
Though it must come by doom,
This quiet comes by kindness too,
And brings me nearer home,

For as I walk the wooded land
The morning of God's mercy,
Beyond the work of mortal hand,
Seen by more than I see,

The quiet deer look up and wait,
Held still in quick of grace.
And I wait, stop footstep and thought.
We stand here face to face.

III

Great deathly powers have passed:
The black and bitter cold, the wind
That broke and felled strong trees, the rind
Of ice that held at last

Even the fleshly heart
In cold that made it seem a stone.
And now there comes again the one
First Sabbath light, the Art

That unruled, uninvoked,
Unknown, makes new again and heals,
Restores heart's flesh so that it feels
Anew the old deadlocked

Goodness of its true home
That it will lose again and mourn,
Remembering the year reborn
In almost perfect bloom

In almost shadeless wood,
Sweet air that neither burned nor chilled
In which the tenderest flowers prevailed,
The light made flesh and blood.

IV

The frog with lichened back and golden thigh
Sits still, almost invisible
On leafed and lichened stem,
Invisibility
Its sign of being at home
There in its given place, and well.

The warbler with its quivering striped throat
Would live almost beyond my sight,
Almost beyond belief,
But for its double note—
Among high leaves a leaf,
At ease, at home in air and light.

And I, through woods and fields, through fallen days
Am passing to where I belong:
At home, at ease, and well,
In Sabbaths of this place
Almost invisible,
Toward which I go from song to song.

V

Six days of work are spent
To make a Sunday quiet
That Sabbath may return.
It comes in unconcern;
We cannot earn or buy it.
Suppose rest is not sent
Or comes and goes unknown,
The light, unseen, unshown.
Suppose the day begins
In wrath at circumstance,
Or anger at one's friends
In vain self-innocence
False to the very light,
Breaking the sun in half,
Or anger at oneself
Whose controverting will
Would have the sun stand still.
The world is lost in loss
Of patience; the old curse
Returns, and is made worse
As newly justified.
In hopeless fret and fuss,
In rage at worldly plight
Creation is defied,
All order is unpropped,
All light and singing stopped.

VI

The intellect so ravenous to know
And in its knowing hold the very light,
Disclosing what is so and what not so,

Must finally know the dark, which is its right
And liberty; it's blind in what it sees.
Bend down, go in by this low door, despite

The thorn and briar that bar the way. The trees
Are young here in the heavy undergrowth
Upon an old field worn out by disease

Of human understanding; greed and sloth
Did bad work that this thicket now conceals,
Work lost to rain or ignorance or both.

The young trees make a darkness here that heals,
And here the forms of human thought dissolve
Into the living shadow that reveals

All orders made by mortal hand or love
Or thought come to a margin of their kind,
Are lost in order we are ignorant of,

Which stirs great fear and sorrow in the mind.
The field, if it will thrive, must do so by
Exactitude of thought, by skill of hand,

And by the clouded mercy of the sky;
It is a mortal clarity between
Two darks, of Heaven and of earth. The why

Of it is *our* measure. Seen and unseen,
Its causes shape it as it is, a while.
O bent by fear and sorrow, now bend down,

Leave word and argument, be dark and still,
And come into the joy of healing shade.
Rest from your work. Be still and dark until

You grow as unopposing, unafraid
As the young trees, without thought or belief;
Until the shadow Sabbath light has made

Shudders, breaks open, shines in every leaf.

1981

1981

I

Here where the world is being made,
No human hand required,
A man may come, somewhat afraid
Always, and somewhat tired,

For he comes ignorant and alone
From work and worry of
A human place, in soul and bone
The ache of human love.

He may come and be still, not go
Toward any chosen aim
Or stay for what he thinks is so.
Setting aside his claim

On all things fallen in his plight,
his mind may move with leaves,
Wind-shaken, in and out of light,
And live as the light lives,

And live as the Creation sings
In covert, two clear notes,
And waits; then two clear answerings
Come from more distant throats—

May live a while with light, shaking
In high leaves, or delayed
In halts of song, submit to making,
The shape of what is made.

1982

I

Dream ended, I went out, awake
To new snow fallen in the dark,
Stainless on road and field, no track
Yet printed on my day of work.

I heard the wild ones muttering,
Assent their dark arrival made
At dawn, gray dawn on dawn-gray wing
Outstretched, shadowless in that shade,

Down from high distances arrived
Within the shelter of the hill;
The river shuddered as they cleaved
Its surface, floated, and were still.

II

Here where the dark-sourced stream brims up,
Reflecting daylight, making sound
In its stepped fall from cup to cup
Of tumbled rocks, singing its round

From cloud to sea to cloud, I climb
The deer road through the leafless trees
Under a wind that batters limb
On limb, still roaring as it has

Two nights and days, cold in slow spring.
But ancient song in a wild throat
Recalls itself and starts to sing
In storm-cleared light; and the bloodroot,

Twinleaf, and rue anemone
Among bare shadows rise, keep faith
With what they have been and will be
Again: frail stem and leaf, mere breath

Of white and starry bloom, each form
Recalling itself to its place
And time. Give thanks, for no windstorm
Or human wrong has altered this,

The forfeit Garden that recalls
Itself here, where both we and it
Belong; no act or thought rebels
In this brief Sabbath now, time fit

To be eternal. Such a bliss
Of bloom's no ornament, but root
And light, a saving loveliness,
Starred firmament here underfoot.

III

The pasture, bleached and cold two weeks ago,
Begins to grow in the spring light and rain;
The new grass trembles under the wind's flow.
The flock, barn-weary, comes to it again,
New to the lambs, a place their mothers know,
Welcoming, bright, and savory in its green,
So fully does the time recover it.
Nibbles of pleasure go all over it.

IV

Thrush song, stream song, holy love
That flows through earthly forms and folds,
The song of Heaven's Sabbath fleshed
In throat and ear, in stream and stone,
A grace living here as we live,
Move my mind now to that which holds
Things as they change.
                                        The warmth has come.
The doors have opened. Flower and song
Embroider ground and air, lead me
Beside the healing field that waits;
Growth, death, and a restoring form
Of human use will make it well.
But I go on, beyond, higher
In the hill's fold, forget the time
I come from and go to, recall
This grove left out of all account,
A place enclosed in song.
                                        Design
Now falls from thought. I go amazed
Into the maze of a design
That mind can follow but not know,
Apparent, plain, and yet unknown,
The outline lost in earth and sky.
What form wakens and rumples this?
Be still. A man who seems to be
A gardener rises out of the ground,
Stands like a tree, shakes off the dark,
The bluebells opening at his feet,
The light a figured cloth of song.

V

To Mary

A child unborn, the coming year
Grows big within us, dangerous,
And yet we hunger as we fear
For its increase: the blunted bud

To free the leaf to have its day,
The unborn to be born. The ones
Who are to come are on their way,
And though we stand in mortal good

Among our dead, we turn in doom
In joy to welcome them, stirred by
That Ghost who stirs in seed and tomb,
Who brings the stones to parenthood.

VI

To Den

We have walked so many times, my boy,
over these old fields given up
to thicket, have thought
and spoken of their possibilities,
theirs and ours, ours and theirs the same,
so many times, that now when I walk here
alone, the thought of you goes with me;
my mind reaches toward yours
across the distance and through time.

No mortal mind's complete within itself,
but minds must speak and answer,
as ours must, on the subject of this place,
our history here, summoned
as we are to the correction
of old wrong in this soil, thinned
and broken, and in our minds.

You have seen on these gullied slopes
the piles of stones mossy with age,
dragged out of furrows long ago
by men now names on stones,
who cleared and broke these fields,
saw them go to ruin, learned nothing
from the trees they saw return
to hold the ground again.

But here is a clearing we have made
at no cost to the world
and to our gain—a *re*-clearing

after forty years: the thicket
cut level with the ground,
grasses and clovers sown
into the last year's fallen leaves,
new pasture coming to the sun
as the woods plants, lovers of shade,
give way: change made
without violence to the ground.

At evening birdcall
flares at the woods' edge;
flight arcs into the opening
before nightfall.

Out of disordered history
a little coherence, a pattern
comes, like the steadying
of a rhythm on a drum, melody
coming to it from time
to time, waking over it,
as from a bird at dawn
or nightfall, the long outline
emerging through the momentary,
as the hill's hard shoulder
shows through trees
when the leaves fall.

The field finds its source
in the old forest, in the thicket
that returned to cover it,
in the dark wilderness of its soil,
in the dispensations of the sky,

in our time, in our minds—
the righting of what was done wrong.

Wrong was easy; gravity helped it.
Right is difficult and long.
In choosing what is difficult
we are free, the mind too
making its little flight
out from the shadow into the clear
in time between work and sleep.

There are two healings: nature's,
and ours and nature's. Nature's
will come in spite of us, after us,
over the graves of its wasters, as it comes
to the forsaken fields. The healing
that is ours and nature's will come
if we are willing, if we are patient,
if we know the way, if we will do the work.
My father's father, whose namesake
you are, told my father this, he told me,
and I am telling you: we make
this healing, the land's and ours:
it is our possibility. We may keep
this place, and be kept by it.
There is a mind of such an artistry
that grass will follow it,
and heal and hold, feed beasts
who will feed us and feed the soil.

Though we invite, this healing comes
in answer to another voice than ours;

a strength not ours returns
out of death beginning in our work.

Though the spring is late and cold,
though uproar of greed
and malice shudders in the sky,
pond, stream, and treetop raise
their ancient songs;
the robin molds her mud nest
with her breast; the air
is bright with breath
of bloom, wise loveliness that asks
nothing of the season but to be.

VII

The clearing rests in song and shade.
It is a creature made
By old light held in soil and leaf,
By human joy and grief,
By human work,
Fidelity of sight and stroke,
By rain, by water on
The parent stone.

We join our work to Heaven's gift,
Our hope to what is left,
That field and woods at last agree
In an economy
Of widest worth.
High Heaven's Kingdom come on earth.
Imagine Paradise.
O dust, arise!

VIII

To Tanya

Our household for the time made right,
All right around us on the hill
For time and for this time, tonight,
Two kernels folded in one shell,

We're joined in sleep beyond desire
To one another and to time,
Whatever time will take or spare,
Forest, field, house, and hollow room

All joined to us, to darkness joined,
All barriers down, and we are borne
Darkly, by thoroughfares unsigned
Toward light we come in time to learn,

In faith no better sighted yet
Than when we plighted first by hope,
By vows more solemn than we thought,
Ourselves to this combining sleep

A quarter century ago,
Lives given to each other and
To time, to lives we did not know
Already given, heart and hand.

Would I come to this time this way
Again, now that I know, confess
So much, knowing I cannot say
More now than then what will be? Yes.

May 29, 1957   May 29, 1982

IX

Hail to the forest born again,
that by neglect, the American benevolence,
has returned to semi-virginity, graceful
in the putrid air, the corrosive rain,
the ash-fall of Heaven-invading fire—
our time's genius to mine the light
of the world's ancient buried days
to make it poisonous in the air.
Light and greed together make a smudge
that stifles and blinds. But here
the light of Heaven's sun descends,
stained and mingled with its forms,
heavy trunk and limb, light leaf and wing,
that we must pray for clarity to see,
not raw sources, symbols, worded powers,
but fellow presences, independent, called
out of nothing by no word of ours,
blessèd, here with us.

X

The dark around us, come,
Let us meet here together,
Members one of another,
Here in our holy room,

Here on our little floor,
Here in the daylit sky,
Rejoicing mind and eye,
Rejoining known and knower,

Light, leaf, foot, hand, and wing,
Such order as we know,
One household, high and low,
And all the earth shall sing.

1983

I

In a crease of the hill
under the light,
out of the wind,
as warmth, bloom, and song
return, lady, I think of you,
and of myself with you.
What are we but forms
of the self-acknowledging
light that brings us
warmth and song from time
to time? Lip and flower,
hand and leaf, tongue
and song, what are we but welcomers
of that ancient joy, always
coming, always passing?
Mayapples rising
out of old time, leaves
folded down around
the stems, as if for flight,
flower bud folded in
unfolding leaves, what
are we but hosts
of times, of all
the Sabbath morning shows,
the light that finds it good.

II

The year relents, and free
Of work, I climb again
To where the old trees wait,
Time out of mind. I hear
Traffic down on the road,
Engines high overhead.
And then a quiet comes,
A cleft in time, silence
Of metal moved by fire;
The air holds little voices,
Titmice and chickadees,
Feeding through the treetops
Among the new small leaves,
Calling again to mind
The grace of circumstance,
Sabbath economy
In which all thought is song,
All labor is a dance.
The world is made at rest,
In ease of gravity.
I hear the ancient theme
In low world-shaping song
Sung by the falling stream.
Here where a rotting log
Has slowed the flow: a shelf
Of dark soil, level laid
Above the tumbled stone.
Roots fasten it in place.
It will be here a while;
What holds it here decays.

A richness from above,
Brought down, is held, and holds
A little while in flow.
Stem and leaf grow from it.
At cost of death, it has
A life. Thus falling founds,
Unmaking makes the world.

III

Now though the season warms
The woods inherits harms
Of human enterprise.
Our making shakes the skies
And taints the atmosphere.
We have ourselves to fear.
We burn the world to live;
Our living blights the leaf.

A clamor high above
Entered the shadowed grove,
Withdrew, was still, and then
The water thrush began
The song that is a prayer,
A form made in the air,
That all who live here pray,
The Sabbath of our day.

May our kind live to breathe
Air worthy of the breath
Of all singers that sing
In joy of their making,
Light of the risen year,
Songs worthy of the ear
Of breathers worth their air,
Of workers worth their hire.

IV

Who makes a clearing makes a work of art,
The true world's Sabbath trees in festival
Around it. And the stepping stream, a part
Of Sabbath also, flows past, by its fall
Made musical, making the hillslope by
Its fall, and still at rest in falling, song
Rising. The field is made by hand and eye,
By daily work, by hope outreaching wrong,
And yet the Sabbath, parted, still must stay
In the dark mazings of the soil no hand
May light, the great Life, broken, make its way
Along the stemmy footholds of the ant.
    Bewildered in our timely dwelling place,
    Where we arrive by work, we stay by grace.

1984

I

Over the river in loud flood,
in the wind deep and broad
under the unending sky, pair
by pair, the swallows again,
with tender exactitude,
play out their line
in arcs laid on the air,
as soon as made, not there.

II

A tired man leaves his labor, felt
In every ligament, to walk
Alone across the new-mowed field,
And at its bound, the last cut stalk,

He takes a road much overgone
In time by bearers of his name,
Though now where foot and hoof beat stone
And passed to what their toil became,

Trees stand that in their long leaf-fall,
Untroubled on forgiving ground,
Have buried the sledged stone with soil
So that his passing makes no sound.

He turns aside, and joins his quiet
Forebears in absence from that way.
He passes through the dappled light
And shadow that the breeze makes sway

Upon him and around him as
He goes. Within the day's design
The leaves sway, darkly, or ablaze
Around their edges with a line

Of fire caught from the sun. He steps
Amid a foliage of song
No tone of which has passed his lips.
Watching, silent, he shifts among

The shiftings of the day, himself
A shifting of the day's design
Whose outline is in doubt, unsafe,
And dark. One time, less learned in pain,

He thought the earth was firm, his own,
But now he knows that all not raised
By fire, by water is brought down.
The slope his fields lie on is poised

Above the river in mere air,
The breaking forewall of a wave,
And everything he has made there
Floats lightly on that fall. To save

What passes is a passing hope
Within the day's design outlawed.
His passing now has brought him up
Into a place not reached by road,

Beyond all history that he knows,
Where trees like great saints stand in time,
Eternal in their patience. Loss
Has rectified the songs that come

Into this columned room, and he
Only in silence, nothing in hand,
Comes here. A generosity
Is here by which the fallen stand.

In history many-named, in time
Nameless, this amplitude conveys

The answering to the asking rhyme
Among confusions that dispraise

The membering name that Adam spoke
By gift, and then heard parceled out
Among all fallen things that croak
And cry and sing and curse and shout.

The foliage opens like a cloud.
At rest high on the valley side,
Silent, the man looks at the loud
World: road and farm, his daily bread,

His beasts, his garden, and his barns,
His trees, the white walls of his house,
Whose lives and hopes he knows. He yearns
Toward all his work has joined. What has

He by his making made but home,
A present help by passing grace
Allowed to creatures of his name
Here in this passing time and place?

III

The crop must drink; we move the pipe
To draw the water back in time
To fall again upon the field,
So that the harvest may grow ripe,
The year complete its ancient rhyme
With other years, and a good yield
Complete our human hope. And this
Is Sunday work, necessity
Depriving us of needed rest.
Yet this necessity is less,
Being met, not by one, but three.
Neighbors, we make this need our feast.

IV

The summer ends, and it is time
To face another way. Our theme
Reversed, we harvest the last row
To store against the cold, undo
The garden that will be undone.
We grieve under the weakened sun
To see all earth's green fountains dried,
And fallen all the works of light.
You do not speak, and I regret
This downfall of the good we sought
As though the fault were mine. I bring
The plow to turn the shattering
Leaves and bent stems into the dark,
From which they may return. At work,
I see you leaving our bright land,
The last cut flowers in your hand.

V

Estranged by distance, he relearns
The way to quiet not his own,
The light at rest on tree and stone,
The high leaves falling in their turns,

Spiraling through the air made gold
By their slow fall. Bright on the ground
They wait their darkening, commend
To coming light the light they hold.

His own long comedown from the air
Complete, safe home again, absence
Withdrawing from him tense by tense
In presence of the resting year,

Blessing and blessed in this result
Of times not blessed, now he has risen.
He walks in quiet beyond division
In surcease of his own tumult.

1985

I

Not again in this flesh will I see
the old trees stand here as they did,
weighty creatures made of light, delight
of their making straight in them and well,
whatever blight our blindness was or made,
however thought or act might fail.

The burden of absence grows, and I pay
daily the grief I owe to love
for women and men, days and trees
I will not know again. Pray
for the world's light thus borne away.
Pray for the little songs that wake and move.

For comfort as these lights depart,
recall again the angels of the thicket,
columbine aerial in the whelming tangle,
song drifting down, light rain, day
returning in song, the lordly Art
piecing out its humble way.

Though blindness may yet detonate in light,
ruining all, after all the years, great right
subsumed at last in paltry wrong,
what do we know? Still
the Presence that we come into with song
is here, shaping the seasons of His wild will.

II

A gracious Sabbath stood here while they stood
Who gave our rest a haven.
Now fallen, they are given
To labor and distress.
These times we know much evil, little good
To steady us in faith
And comfort when our losses press
Hard on us, and we choose,
In panic or despair or both,
To keep what we will lose.

For we are fallen like the trees, our peace
Broken, and so we must
Love where we cannot trust,
Trust where we cannot know,
And must await the wayward-coming grace
That joins living and dead,
Taking us where we would not go—
Into the boundless dark.
When what was made has been unmade
The Maker comes to His work.

III

Awaked from the persistent dream
Of human chaos come again,
I walk in the lamed woods, the light
Brought down by felling of great trees,
And in the rising thicket where
The shadow of old grace returns.
Leaf shadows tremble on light leaves,
A lighter foliage of song
Among them, the wind's thousand tongues,
And songs of birds. Beams reaching down
Into the shadow swirl and swarm
With gleaming traffic of the air,
Bright grains of generative dust
And winged intelligences. Among
High maple leaves a spider's wheel
Shines, work of finest making made
Touchingly in the dark.
                              The dark
Again has prayed the light to come
Down into it, to animate
And move it in its heaviness.

So what was still and dark wakes up,
Becomes intelligent, moves, names
Itself by hunger and by kind,
Walks, swims, flies, cries, calls, speaks, or sings.
We all are praising, praying to
The light we are, but cannot know.

IV

The fume and shock and uproar
of the internal combustion of America
recede, the last vacationers gone
back to the life that drives away from home.

Bottles and wrappers of expensive
cheap feasts ride the quieted current
toward the Gulf of Mexico.

And now the breeze comes down
from the hill, the kingfisher returns
to the dead limb of the sycamore,
the swallows feed in the air
over the water.

        A muskrat draws his V
under the lowhanging willows.
In clear shallows near the rocks
tiny fish flicker and soar. A dove
sweetens the distance with his call.

Out of the frenzy of an August Sunday
the Sabbath comes. The valley glows.
A raincrow flies across the river
into the shadowy leaves. The dark falls.

V

How long does it take to make the woods?
As long as it takes to make the world.
The woods is present as the world is, the presence
of all its past, and of all its time to come.
It is always finished, it is always being made, the act
of its making forever greater than the act of its destruction.
It is a part of eternity, for its end and beginning
belong to the end and beginning of all things,
the beginning lost in the end, the end in the beginning.

What is the way to the woods, how do you go there?
By climbing up through the six days' field,
kept in all the body's years, the body's
sorrow, weariness, and joy. By passing through
the narrow gate on the far side of that field
where the pasture grass of the body's life gives way
to the high, original standing of the trees.
By coming into the shadow, the shadow
of the grace of the strait way's ending,
the shadow of the mercy of light.

Why must the gate be narrow?
Because you cannot pass beyond it burdened.
To come in among these trees you must leave behind
the six days' world, all of it, all of its plans and hopes.
You must come without weapon or tool, alone,
expecting nothing, remembering nothing,
into the ease of sight, the brotherhood of eye and leaf.

VI

Life forgives its depredations;
new-shaped by loss, goes on.
Luther Penn, our neighbor
still in our minds, will not
come down to the creek mouth to fish
in April anymore. The year
ripens. Leaves fall. In openings
where old trees were cut down,
showing the ground to the sky,
snakeroot blooms white,
giving shine unto the world.
Ant and beetle scuttle through
heroic passages, go to dust;
their armor tumbles in the mold.
Broad wings enter the grove, fold
and are still, open and go.

VII

The winter wren is back, quick
Among the treeroots by the stream,
Feeding from stem to stone to stick,
And in his late return the rhyme

Of years again completes itself.
He makes his work a kind of play.
He pauses on a little shelf
Of rock, says "Tick!" and flirts away,

Too busy in that other world
His hungry vision brings to sight
To be afraid. He makes a gnarled
Root graceful with his airy weight,

Breathes in the great informing Breath,
Made little in his wing and eye,
And breathes it out again in deft
Bright links of song, his clarity.

1986

I

Slowly, slowly, they return
To the small woodland let alone:
Great trees, outspreading and upright,
Apostles of the living light.

Patient as stars, they build in air
Tier after tier a timbered choir,
Stout beams upholding weightless grace
Of song, a blessing on this place.

They stand in waiting all around,
Uprisings of their native ground,
Downcomings of the distant light;
They are the advent they await.

Receiving sun and giving shade,
Their life's a benefaction made,
And is a benediction said
Over the living and the dead.

In fall their brightened leaves, released,
Fly down the wind, and we are pleased
To walk on radiance, amazed.
O light come down to earth, be praised!

1987

I

Coming to the woods' edge
on my Sunday morning walk,
I stand resting a moment beside
a ragged half-dead wild plum
in bloom, its perfume
a moment enclosing me,
and standing side by side
with the old broken blooming tree,
I almost understand,
I almost recognize as a friend
the great impertinence of beauty
that comes even to the dying,
even to the fallen, without reason
sweetening the air.

                I walk on,
distracted by a letter accusing me
of distraction, which distracts me
only from the hundred things
that would otherwise distract me
from this whiteness, lightness,
sweetness in the air. The mind
is broken by the thousand
calling voices it is always too late
to answer, and that is why it yearns
for some hard task, lifelong, longer
than life, to concentrate it
and make it whole.

But where is the all-welcoming,
all-consecrating Sabbath
that would do the same? Where
the quietness of the heart
and the eye's clarity
that would be a friend's reply
to the white-blossoming plum tree?

II

I climb up through the thicket,
a bird's song somewhere within it,
the singer unfound within the song
resounding within itself and around
itself; it might come from anywhere,
from everywhere, the whole air
vibrant with it, every leaf a tongue.

*

I reach the last stand in my going
of woodland never felled, a little patch
of trees on ground too poor to plow, spared
the belittlement of human intention
from time before human thought. They bring
that time to mind: their long standing, and
our longing to understand. But a man
is small before those who have stood so long.
He stands under them, looks up, sees, knows,
and knows he does not know.

*

Explanations topple into their events,
merely other events, smaller and less
significant. They disappear, or die away
like little cries at sundown, and the old trees
receive the night again in dignity
and patience, present beyond the complex
lineages of cause and effect, each one

lost to us in what it is. For us, the privilege
is only to see, within the long shade,
the present standing of what has come and is
to come: the straight trunks aspiring
between earth and sky, bearing upon all years
the year's new leaves.

*

               Or we may see
this valley as from above and outside,
as from a distance off in time, as Cézanne
might have seen it: the light
stopped, at rest in its scintillation
on the bright strokes of the leaves
also at rest, sight and light entering
from the same direction, so that we see it
shadowless, for all time, forever.

*

I come to a little bench, a mere shelf
of the slope, where four deer slept the night,
and I lie down in the deer's bed
and, warm in my old jacket in the cold
morning of late April, sleep a sleep as dark
and vast as the deer slept, or as the dead sleep,
simple and dreamless in their graves,
awaiting the dawn that will stand them
timeless as they stood in time, and at last
open my eyes to the bright sky, the luminous
small new leaves unfolding.

III

And now the lowland grove is down, the trees
Fallen that had unearthly power to please
The earthly eye, and gave unearthly solace
To minds grown quiet in that quiet place.
To see them standing was to know a prayer
Prayed to the Holy Spirit in the air
By that same Spirit dwelling in the ground.
The wind in their high branches gave the sound
Of air replying to that prayer. The rayed
Imperial light sang in the leaves it made.

To live as mourner of a human friend
Is but to understand the common end
Told by the steady counting in the wrist.
For though the absent friend is mourned and missed
At every pulse, it is a human loss
In human time made well; our grief will bless
At last the dear lost flesh and breath; it will
Grow quiet as the body in the hill.

To live to mourn an ancient woodland, known
Always, loved with an old love handed down,
That is a grief that will outlast the griever,
Grief as landmark, grief as a wearing river
That in its passing stays, biding in rhyme
Of year with year, time with returning time,
As though beyond the grave the soul will wait
In long unrest the shaping of the light
In branch and bole through centuries that prepare
This ground to pray again its finest prayer.

IV

May what I've written here
In sleepless grief and dread
Live in my children's ears
To warn them of their need
And ask them to forbear
In time when I am dead

So they may look and see
For past and future's sake
The terms of victory
They cannot win or take
Except by charity
Toward what they cannot make.

V

And now the remnant groves grow bright with praise.
They light around me like an old man's days.

VI

Remembering that it happened once,
We cannot turn away the thought,
As we go out, cold, to our barns
Toward the long night's end, that we
Ourselves are living in the world
It happened in when it first happened,
That we ourselves, opening a stall
(A latch thrown open countless times
Before), might find them breathing there,
Foreknown: the Child bedded in straw,
The mother kneeling over Him,
The husband standing in belief
He scarcely can believe, in light
That lights them from no source we see,
An April morning's light, the air
Around them joyful as a choir.
We stand with one hand on the door,
Looking into another world
That is this world, the pale daylight
Coming just as before, our chores
To do, the cattle all awake,
Our own white frozen breath hanging
In front of us; and we are here
As we have never been before,
Sighted as not before, our place
Holy, although we knew it not.

1988

I

Now I have reached the age
of judgment giving sorrow
that many men have come to,
the verdict of regret,
remembering the world
once better than it is,
my old walkways beneath
the vanished trees, and friends
lost now in loss of trust.

And I recall myself
more innocent than I am,
gone past coming back
in the history of flaw,
except Christ dead and risen
in my own flesh shall judge,
condemn, and then forgive.

II

It is the destruction of the world
in our own lives that drives us
half insane, and more than half.
To destroy that which we were given
in trust: how will we bear it?
It is our own bodies that we give
to be broken, our bodies
existing before and after us
in clod and cloud, worm and tree,
that we, driving or driven, despise
in our greed to live, our haste
to die. To have lost, wantonly,
the ancient forests, the vast grasslands
is our madness, the presence
in our very bodies of our grief.

III

Another year has returned us
to the day of our marriage
thirty-one years ago. Many times
we have known, and again forgot
in our cruel separateness,
that making touch that feelingly
persuades us what we are:
one another's and many others',
brought together as by a music
of singing birds hidden among
the leaves, or the memory of
small flowers in the dark grass.
How strange to think of children
yet to come, into whose making we
will be made, who will not know us
even so little as we know
ourselves, who have already gone
so far beyond our own recall.

IV

The world of machines is running
Beyond the world of trees
Where only a leaf is turning
In a small high breeze.

V

Always in the distance
the sound of cars is passing
on the road, that simplest form
going only two ways,
both ways away. And I
have been there in that going.

But now I rest and am
apart, a part of the form
of the woods always arriving
from all directions home,
this cell of wild sound,
the hush of the trees, singers
hidden among the leaves—

a form whose history is old,
needful, unknown, and bright
as the history of the stars
that tremble in the sky at night
like leaves of a great tree.

1989

I

In early morning we awaken from
The sound of engines running in the night,
And then we start the engines of the day.
We speed away into the fading light.

Nowhere is any sound but of our going
On roads strung everywhere with humming wire.
Nowhere is there an end except in smoke.
This is the world that we have set on fire.

This is the promised burning, darkening
Our light of hope and putting out the sun,
Blighting the leaf, the stream—and blessed are
The dead who died before this time began.

Blessed the dead who have escaped in time
The twisted metal and the fractured stone,
The technobodies of the hopeless cure.
Now, to the living, only grief has shown

The little yellow of the violet
Risen again out of the dead year's leaves,
And grief alone is measure of the love
That only lives by rising out of graves.

II

The old oak wears new leaves.
It stands for many lives.
Within its veil of green
A singer sings unseen.
Again the living come
To light, and are at home.
And Edward Abbey's gone.
I pass a cairn of stone
Two arm-lengths long and wide
Piled on the steep hillside
By plowmen years ago.
Now oaks and hickories grow
Where the steel coulter passed.
Where human striving ceased
The Sabbath of the trees
Returns and stands and is.
The leaves shake in the wind.
I think of that dead friend
Here where he never came
Except by thought and name;
I praise the joyous rage
That justified his page.
He would have liked this place
Where spring returns with solace
Of bloom in a dark time,
Larkspur and columbine.
The flute song of the thrush
Sounds in the underbrush.

III

Now Loyce Flood is dead,
A stone is at her head,
The green sod over her,
The snow will cover her.
Owen lay in that place,
The commonwealth of peace,
Fifteen years to the day
Before she came to stay.
We left them there together,
Safe now from time and weather,
At rest as man and wife.
I thank them for the life
That they in marriage made,
Faithful and unafraid,
Frugal and bountiful.
May what was beautiful
In all they said and did
Or thought and left unsaid
Flow to them like a river
And comfort them forever.

IV

He thought to keep himself from Hell
by knowing and by loving well.
His work and vision, his desire
Would keep him climbing up the stair.

At limit now of flesh and bone,
He cannot climb for holding on.
"I fear the drop, I feel the blaze—
Lord, grant thy mercy and thy grace."

V

One morning out of time,
The final darkness passed, I wake
And rise, my body light,
light all around. For the light's sake

I walk a narrow path
Through a steep woodland that I know,
Older and younger than
I knew, untainted by the sorrow

That I recall to find
It is not there. The light has made
A perfect greenness there,
Birdsong cascading through the shade.

Nearby there is a town
Of few houses and many graves,
Which now have filled with light.
Where love has equaled grief, who grieves?

I meet a man I've known
Always, though memory recalls
No name, a man both old
And young, dressed in clean overalls,

Who nudges his hat brim
Upward with one thumb to show me
His face. "It's Burley Coulter,
Andy. Andy, don't you know me?"

VI

(Massachusetts Avenue at Rock Creek Park)

Here by the road where people are carried, with
or against their will, as on a river of burning oil
through a time already half consumed, how
shall we pray to escape the catastrophe
that we have not the vision to oppose and have
therefore deserved, and that many have desired?

Yet here in our moment in the ages of ages
amid the icons of fire from the maddened center
whirling out, we pray to be delivered from the blaze
that we have earned, that many desire. We pray
that the continent of love may be shaped within
the continent of power, here by the river of fire.

We pray for vision, though we die, to see
in our small imperfect love the Love of the ages
of ages, whose green tree yet stands amid the flames. May we
be as a song sung within the tree, though beside us
the river of oil flows, burning, and the sky is filled
with the whine of desire to burn and be burned in the fire.

VII

The sky bright after summer-ending rain,
I sat against an oak half up the climb.
The sun was low; the woods was hushed in shadow;
Now the long shimmer of the crickets' song
Had stopped. I looked up to the westward ridge
And saw the ripe October light again,
Shining through leaves still green yet turning gold.
Those glowing leaves made of the light a place
That time and leaf would leave. The wind came cool,
And then I knew that I was present in
The long age of the passing world, in which
I once was not, now am, and will not be,
And in that time, beneath the changing tree,
I rested in a keeping not my own.

VIII

One day I walked imagining
What work I might do here,
The place, once dark, made clear
By work and thought, my managing,
The world thus made more dear.
I walked and dreamed, the sun in clouds,
Dreamer and day at odds.

The world in its great mystery
Was hidden by my dream.
Today I make no claim;
I dream of what is here, the tree
Beside the falling stream,
The stone, the light upon the stone;
And day and dream are one.

1990

I

The two, man and boy, wait
by their lantern, the hounds already
loose in the nearby dark.
The man calls again: "Oh, Mart!"
Soon, near the lighted window
of an invisible house beyond
the flooded creek, another light
appears, moving with the motion
of a man walking. It slants down
along the far slope, steps
onto swinging footboards
strung above the flood, crosses
slowly, swaying with the sways
of the lithe bridge, bends
around by the old road
and up the bank. Having traced
so far a man's way in this
dark world, the lantern lifts
to light the faces of the two
and of its bearer. "*Yes*sir!
How you fellows this evenin?"

*

And so I came to know
The light borne in this world
By Martin Rowanberry,
Who knew no enemy,
And yet was killed by hate.
Beside the opened grave,
The hillside white with snow,

Hope makes its little song:
"And we will see him in
The morning over there."
The voices cease. And we
Can do no more for him.
The light he was returns
Unto the Light that is.

*

Though now he has no time
For us, he stays with us
In time—a good in us
Learned from the good in him.

*

Today the cold rain falls,
A north wind shakes the walls,
The sound earth turns to mud.
The river in brown flood
Will not return the clay
It lifts and bears away.
Now may love equal fear,
As death begins the year.

II

To give mind to machines, they are calling it
out of the world, out of the neighborhood, out of the body.
They have bound it in the brain, in the hard shell
of the skull, in order to bind it in a machine.

From the heron flying home at dusk,
from the misty hollows at sunrise,
from the stories told at the row's end,
they are calling the mind into exile
in the dry circuits of machines.

III

After the slavery of the body, dumbfoundment
of the living flesh in the order of spending
and wasting, then comes the enslavement
of consciousness, the incarnation of mind
in machines. Once the mind is reduced
to the brain, then it falls within the grasp
of the machine. It is the mind incarnate
in the body, in community, and in the earth
that they cannot confine. The difference
is love; the difference is grief and joy.
Remember the body's pleasure and its sorrow.
Remember its grief at the loss of all it knew.
Remember its redemption in suffering
and in love. Remember its resurrection
on the last day, when all made things
that have not refused this passage
will return, clarified, each fully being
in the being of all. Remember the small
secret creases of the earth—the grassy,
the wooded, and the rocky—that the water
has made, finding its way. Remember
the voices of the water flowing. Remember
the water flowing under the shadows
of the trees, of the tall grasses, of the stones.
Remember the water striders walking over
the surface of the water as it flowed.
Remember the great sphere of the small
wren's song, through which the water flowed
and the light fell. Remember, and come to rest
in light's ordinary miracle.

IV

I walk in openings
That when I'm dead will close.
Where the field sparrow sings
Will come the sweet wild rose.

The yellowthroat will claim
The tangle with his song,
The redbud and wild plum
Light up the hill in spring

Where in the morning shade
My team of horses drew
The chattering iron blade,
Their fetlocks wet with dew.

Briar, bittersweet, and fern,
Box elder, locust, elm,
Cedar, wild grape, and thorn
Will reinstate the time

Of deep root and wide shadow,
Of bright, hot August calm
On the small, tree-ringed meadow
Of goldenrod and bee balm.

Thicket will grow up through
The thatches of the grass,
An old way turning new
As lives and wishes pass.

And as the thicket dies
The hickory, ash, and oak
Of the true woods will rise;
Across a long time, like

Will speak to like, the breeze
Resume old music in
The branch-ends of the trees,
The long age come again.

The hard field will find ease
In being thus released:
Let it grow wild in peace,
My workplace come to rest.

To speed this change of goods
I spare the seedling trees,
And thus invoke the woods,
The genius of this place;

I stop the mower blade,
And so conspire with time
In the return of shade,
Completion of this rhyme.

V

The body in the invisible
Familiar room accepts the gift
Of sleep, and for a while is still;
Instead of will, it lives by drift

In the great night that gathers up
The earth and sky. Slackened, unbent,
Unwanting, without fear or hope,
The body rests beyond intent.

Sleep is the prayer the body prays,
Breathing in unthought faith the Breath
That through our worry-wearied days
Preserves our rest, and is our truth.

VI

(St. Vith, December 21, 1944)

Cut off in front of the line
that now ran through St. Vith,
the five American tanks sat
in a field covered with snow
in the dark. And now they must
retreat to safety, which they
could do only through gunfire
and flame in the burning town.
They went, firing, through the fire,
GIs and German prisoners
clinging to the hulls, and out
again into the still night beyond.
In the broad dark, someone
began to sing, and one by one
the others sang also, the German
prisoners singing in German,
the Americans in English,
the one song. "Silent night,"
they sang as the great treads
passed on across the dark
countryside muffled in white
snow, "Holy night."

1991

I

The year begins with war.
Our bombs fall day and night,
Hour after hour, by death
Abroad appeasing wrath,
Folly, and greed at home.
Upon our giddy tower
We'd oversway the world.
Our hate comes down to kill
Those whom we do not see,
For we have given up
Our sight to those in power
And to machines, and now
Are blind to all the world.
This is a nation where
No lovely thing can last.
We trample, gouge, and blast;
The people leave the land;
The land flows to the sea.
Fine men and women die,
The fine old houses fall,
The fine old trees come down:
Highway and shopping mall
Still guarantee the right
And liberty to be
A peaceful murderer,
A murderous worshipper,
A slender glutton, or
A healthy whore. Forgiving
No enemy, forgiven

By none, we live the death
Of liberty, become
What we have feared to be.

II

The ewes crowd to the mangers;
Their bellies widen, sag;
Their udders tighten. Soon
The little voices cry
In morning cold. Soon now
The garden must be worked,
Laid off in rows, the seed
Of life to come brought down
Into the dark to rest,
Abide a while alone,
And rise. Soon, soon again
The cropland must be plowed,
For the year's promise now
Answers the year's desire,
Its hunger and its hope.
This goes against the time
When food is bought, not grown.
O come into the market
With cash, and come to rest
In this economy
Where all we need is money
To be well-stuffed and free
By sufferance of our Lord,
The Chairman of the Board.
Because there's thus no need,
There is the greatest need
To plant one's ground with seed.
Under the season's sway,
Against the best advice,
In time of death and tears,

In slow snowfall of years,
Defiant and in hope,
We keep an older way
In light and breath to stay
This household on its slope.

III

Now with its thunder spring
Returns. The river, raised,
Carries the rain away.
Carp wallow in the shoals
Above our flooded fields.
Jonquils return to dooryards
Of vanished houses. Phoebes
Return to build again
Under the stilted porch.
On thicketed hillsides
The young trees bud and bloom;
They stand in poisoned air
In their community.
Twinleaf and bloodroot flower
Out of the fallen leaves.
At flood's edge all night long
The little frogs are singing.
In the dark barn, hard rain
Loud on the roof, long time
Till dawn, the young ewe calls
The lamb yet in her womb.

IV

The team rests in shade at the edge
of the half-harrowed field, the first
warm morning of May. Wind breathes
over the worked ground, through maples
by the creek, moving every new leaf.
The stream sings quietly in passing.
Too late for frost, too early for flies,
the air carries only birdsong, the long
draft of wind through leaves. In this time
I could stay forever. In my wish
to stay forever, it stays forever.
But I must go. Mortal and obliged,
I shake off stillness, stand and go back
to the waiting field, unending rounds.

V

The seed is in the ground.
Now may we rest in hope
While darkness does its work.

VI   The Locusts

Seventeen more years, and they are here
again, having risen up out of the dark,
emerged winged out of their riven shells
to fly in light, to mate and die,
and yet again return, in God's economy
that lets no made thing finally fall.
And we, who vowed ourselves to one another
twice seventeen years ago, know like these
the hard patience of being dark, separate,
and half alive. Like them, from time
to time we rise up, become full grown,
complex, and whole. Become one,
the true person we are pledged to be,
we leave the dark. Mortal and destined,
earthen and winged, we come into the light.

VII

Where the great trees were felled
The thorns and thistles grow
From the unshaded ground,
And so the Fall's renewed
And all the creatures mourn,
Groan and travail in pain
Together until now.
And yet their Maker's here,
Within and over all
Now and forevermore,
Being and yet to be
In columbine, oak tree,
Woodthrush, beetle, and worm,
In song of thrush and stream,
Fact, mystery, and dream:
Spirit in love with form,
And loving to inform
Form formed within itself
As thought, fulfilled in flesh,
And made to live by breath
Breathed into it by love.
The violence past for now,
The felling and the falling
Done, as a mourner walks
Restless from room to room,
I cross the stream to find
On a neglected slope
The woods' floor starred with bloom.

VIII

What do the tall trees say
To the late havocs in the sky?
They sigh.
The air moves, and they sway.
When the breeze on the hill
Is still, then they stand still.
They wait.
They have no fear. Their fate
Is faith. Birdsong
Is all they've wanted, all along.

IX   The Farm

Go by the narrow road
Along the creek, a burrow
Under shadowy trees
Such as a mouse makes through
Tall grass, so that you may
Forget the wide road you
Have left behind, and all
That it has led to. Or,
Best, walk up through the woods,
Around the valley rim,
And down to where the trees
Give way to cleared hillside,
So that you reach the place
Out of the trees' remembrance
Of their kind; seasonal
And timeless, they stand in
Uncounted time, and you
Have passed among them, small
As a mouse at a feast,
Unnoticed at the feet
Of all those mighty guests.
Come on a clear June morning
As the fog lifts, trees drip,
And birds make everywhere
Uninterrupted song.

However you may come,
You'll see it suddenly
Lie open to the light
Amid the woods: a farm

Little enough to see
Or call across—cornfield,
Hayfield, and pasture, clear
As if remembered, dreamed
And yearned for long ago,
Neat as a blossom now
When all its fields are mowed
And dew is fresh upon it,
Bird music all around.
That is the vision, seen
As on a Sabbath walk:
The possibility
Of human life whose terms
Are Heaven's and this earth's.

Stay years if you would know
The work and thought, the pleasure
And grief, the feat, by which
This vision lives. In fall
Or winter you should plow
A patch of bottomland
For corn; the freezes then
Will work the heavy clods.
When it's too wet to plow,
Go to the woods to fell
Trees for next winter's fuel.
Take the inferior trees
And not all from one place,
So that the woods will yield
Without diminishment.
Then trim and rick the logs;
And when you drag them out

From woods to rick, use horses
Whose hooves are kinder to
The ground than wheels. In spring
The traces of your work
Will be invisible.

Near winter's end, your flock
Will bear their lambs, and you
Must be alert, out late
And early at the barn,
To guard against the grief
You cannot help but feel
When any young thing made
For life falters at birth
And dies. Save the best hay
To feed the suckling ewes.
Shelter them in the barn
Until the grass is strong,
Then turn them out to graze
The green hillsides, good pasture
With shade and water close.
Then watch for dogs, whose sport
Will be to kill your sheep
And ruin all your work.
Or old Coyote may
Become your supper guest,
Unasked and without thanks;
He'll just excerpt a lamb
And dine before you know it.
But don't, because of that,
Make war against the world
And its wild appetites.

A guard dog or a donkey
Would be the proper answer;
Or use electric fence.
For you must learn to live
With neighbors never chosen
As with the ones you chose.
Coyote's song at midnight
Says something for the world
The world wants said. And when
You know your flock is safe
You'll like to wake and hear
That wild voice sing itself
Free in the dark, at home.

As the fields dry, complete
Your plowing; you must do this
As early as you can.
Then disk and drag the furrows.
And now the past must come
To serve the future: dung
And straw from the barn floor
You carry to the fields,
Load after load until
The barns are clean, the cropland
All covered with manure.
In early May, prepare
The corn ground, plant the corn.
And now you are committed.
Wait for the seed to sprout,
The green shoots, tightly rolled,
To show above the ground
As risen from the grave.

Then you must cultivate
To keep them free of weeds
Until they have grown tall
And can defend themselves.

Where you grew corn last year,
Sow buckwheat, let it seed,
Then disk it in and grow
A second crop to disk in.
This is for humus, and
To keep out weeds. It is
A Sabbath for the land,
Rest and enrichment, good
For it, for you, for all
The ones who are unborn;
The land must have its Sabbath
Or take it when we starve.
The ground is mellow now,
Friable and porous: rich.
Mid-August is the time
To sow this field in clover
And grass, to cut for hay
Two years, pasture a while,
And then return to corn.

But don't neglect your garden.
Household economy
Makes family and land
An independent state.
Never buy at a store
What you can grow or find
At home—this is the rule

Of liberty, also
Of neighborhood. (And be
Faithful to local merchants
Too. Never buy far off
What you can buy near home.)
As early as you can,
Plant peas, onions, and greens,
Potatoes, radishes,
Cabbage and cauliflower,
Lettuce, carrots, and beets—
Things that will stand the frost.
Then as the weather warms
Plant squashes, corn, and beans,
Okra, tomatoes, herbs,
Flowers—some for yourself
And some to give away.
In the cornfield plant pole beans,
Pumpkins, and winter squash;
Thus by diversity
You can enlarge the yield.

You have good grass and hay,
So keep a cow or two.
Milk made from your own grass
Is cheap and sweet. A cow
To milk's a good excuse
To bring you home from places
You do not want to be.
Fatten the annual calf
For slaughter. Keep a pig
To rescue scraps, skimmed milk,
And other surpluses.

Keep hens who will make eggs
And meat of offal, insects,
A little of your corn.
Eat these good beasts that eat
What you can't eat. Be thankful
To them and to the plants,
To your small, fertile homeland,
To topsoil, light, and rain
That daily give you life.

Be thankful and repay
Growth with good work and care.
Work done in gratitude,
Kindly, and well, is prayer.
You did not make yourself,
Yet you must keep yourself
By use of other lives.
No gratitude atones
For bad use or too much.

This is not work for hire.
By this expenditure
You make yourself a place;
You make yourself a way
For love to reach the ground.
In its ambition and
Its greed, its violence,
The world is turned against
This possibility,
And yet the world survives
By the survival of
This kindly working love.

And while you work your fields
Do not forget the woods.
The woods stands by the field
To measure it, and teach
Its keeper. Nature is
The best farmer, for she
Preserves the land, conserves
The rain; she deepens soil,
Wastes nothing; and she is
Diverse and orderly.
She is our mother, teacher,
And final judge on earth.
The farm's a human order
Opening among the trees,
Remembering the woods.
To farm, live like a tree
That does not grow beyond
The power of its place.
It rises by the strength
Of local soil and light,
Aspiring to no height
That it has not attained.
More time, more light, more rain
Will make it grow again
Till it has realized
All that it can become,
And then it dies into
More life, deserving more
By not desiring more.

The year's first fullness comes
To the hayfields. In May,
Watching the sky, you mow

Your fields before the grass
Toughens and while the clover
Stands in its early bloom.
But weather's iffy here
In May, and in these close
Valleys, the early cutting
Is hard to cure. Some rain
Will fall on swath or windrow,
As like as not, to darken
The hay. "It beats a snowball,"
You say then to console
Yourself, and look ahead
To later cuttings, lighter,
Better, quicker to dry.
In summer, thus, you think
Of winter, load the barns
In heat against the cold,
The January days
When you'll go out to feed,
Your breath a little cloud,
The blue air glittery
With frost. On the tracked snow,
On ground that's frozen hard,
You free the smell of summer
From bales of hay thrown down
Before the hungry stock.

Soon you have salad greens
Out of the garden rows,
Then peas, early potatoes,
Onions, beets, beans, sweet corn.
The bounty of the year
Now comes in like a tide:

Yellow summer squashes,
Pole beans from the cornfield,
Tomatoes, okra, eggplant,
Cabbage and cauliflower.
Eat, and give to the neighbors;
Preserve for wintertime;
Plant more, and fight the weeds.
Later will come the fall crops:
Turnips, parsnips, more greens,
The winter squashes, cushaws,
And pumpkins big as tubs.
"Too much for us," you'll say,
And give some more away.
Or try to; nowadays,
A lot of people would
Rather work hard to buy
Their food already cooked
Than get it free by work.

Best of all is the fruit,
Sweetest and prettiest:
The strawberries and cherries,
The gooseberries and currants,
Raspberries and blackberries
(The best are wild), grapes, pears,
Apples early and late—
These gleamings in the sun
That gleam upon the tongue
And gleam put up in jars
And gleam within the mind.

Of all your harvests, those
Are pleasantest that come

Freest: blackberries from
Wild fencerows; strawberries
You happen on in crossing
The grassy slopes in June;
Wild cherries and wild grapes,
Sour at first taste, then sweet;
Persimmons and blackhaws
That you pick up to eat
On days you walk among
The red and yellow leaves;
And walnuts, hickory nuts
Gathered beneath the trees.
In your wild foragings
The earth feeds you the way
She feeds the beasts and birds.

And all the summer long
You're putting up more hay;
You clip the pastures, keep
The fences up, repair
Your buildings, milk your cows;
You wean the lambs; you move
The livestock to new grass;
And you must walk the fields
With hoe in hand, to cut
The thistles and the docks.
There is no end to work—
Work done in pleasure, grief,
Or weariness, with ease
Of skill and timeliness,
Or awkwardly or wrong,
Too hurried or too slow.
One job completed shows

Another to be done.
And so you make the farm
That must be daily made
And yearly made, or it
Will not exist. If you
Should go and not return
And none should follow you,
This clarity would be
As if it never was.
But praise, in knowing this,
The genius of the place,
Whose ways forgive your own,
And will resume again
In time, if left alone.
You work always in this
Dear opening between
What was and is to be.

And so you make the farm,
And so you disappear
Into your days, your days
Into the ground. Before
You start each day, the place
Is as it is, and at
The day's end, it is as
It is, a little changed
By work, but still itself,
Having included you
And everything you've done.
And it is who you are,
And you are what it is.
You will work many days

No one will ever see;
Their record is the place.
This way you come to know
That something moves in time
That time does not contain.
For by this timely work
You keep yourself alive
As you came into time,
And as you'll leave: God's dust,
God's breath, a little Light.

To rest, go to the woods
Where what is made is made
Without your thought or work.
Sit down; begin the wait
For small trees to grow big,
Feeding on earth and light.
Their good result is song
The winds must bring, that trees
Must wait to sing, and sing
Longer than you can wait.
Soon you must go. The trees,
Your seniors, standing thus
Acknowledged in your eyes,
Stand as your praise and prayer.
Your rest is in this praise
Of what you cannot be
And what you cannot do.

But make your land recall,
In workdays of the fields,
The Sabbath of the woods.

Although your fields must bear
The barbed seed of the Fall,
Though nations yet make war
For madness and for hire,
By work in harmony
With the God-given world
You bring your days to rest,
Remain a living soul.
In time of hate and waste,
Wars and rumors of wars,
Rich armies and poor peace,
Your blessed economy,
Beloved sufficiency
Upon a dear, small place,
Sings with the morning stars.

Autumn ripens the corn.
You pick the yellow ears,
Carry them from the field,
Rich, satisfying loads.
The garden's final yield
Now harvested, the ground
Worked and manured, prepared
For spring, put out of mind,
You must saw, split, bring in,
And store your winter wood.
And thus the year comes round.

X

Loving you has taught me the infinite
longing of the self to be given away
and the great difficulty of that entire
giving, for in love to give is to receive
and then there is yet more to give;
and others have been born of our giving
to whom the self, greatened by gifts,
must be given, and by that giving
be increased, until, self-burdened,
the self, staggering upward in years,
in fear, hope, love, and sorrow,
imagines, rising like a moon,
a pale moon risen in daylight
over the dark woods, the Self
whose gift we and all others are,
the self that is by definition given.

1992

1992

I

The winter world of loss
And grief is gone. The night
Is past. Along the whole
Length of the river, birds
Are singing in the trees.

Again, hope dreams itself
Awake. The year's first lambs
Cry in the morning dark.
And, after all, we have
A garden in our minds.

We living know the worth
Of all the dead have done
Or hoped to do. We know
That hearts, against their doom,
Must plight an ancient troth.

Now come the bride and groom,
Now come the man and woman
Who must begin again
The work divine and human
By which we live on earth.

(Pryor Clifford & Billie Carol—March 7, 1992)

II

Lift up the dead leaves
and see, waiting
in the dark, in cold March,

the purplish stems, leaves,
and buds of twinleaf,
infinitely tender, infinitely

expectant. They straighten
slowly into the light after
the nights of frost. At last

the venture is made: the brief
blossoms open, the petals fall,
the hinged capsules of seed

grow big. The possibility
of this return returns
again to the seed, the dark,

the long wait, and the light again.

III

Again we come
to the resurrection
of bloodroot from the dark,

a hand that reaches up
out of the ground,
holding a lamp.

IV

I went away only
a few hundred steps
up the hill, and turned
and started home.
And then I saw
the pasture green under
the trees, the open
hillside, the little ponds,
our house, cistern,
woodshed, and barn,
the river bending in
its valley, our garden
new-planted beside it.
All around, the woods
that had been stark
in the harsh air
of March, had turned
soft with new leaves.
Birdsong had returned
to the branches:
the stream sang
in the fold of the hill.
In its time and great patience
beauty had come upon us,
greater than I had imagined.

V

I too am not at home
When you are gone
And I am here alone.
Until you come

I am as dead, condemned
To fractionhood,
A stillness of the blood,
Dark in the ground.

But I rise up alive
When you come near
Our place of flowers where
Alone I live.

VI

My sore ran in the night
and ceased not. I tossed to and fro
unto the dawning of the day.
Let the sighs of the prisoner
come before thee; according to
the greatness of thy power
preserve thou those that are
appointed to die. I remembered
my song in the night. I said,
This is my sorrow, but I will
remember the works of the Lord;
I will remember his wonders
of old. And I remembered
the small stream coming down
off the hill through all the years
of my people, and long before.
I remembered the trees on the slopes
beside it, standing in the great heat
of summer, and giving shade.
I remembered the leaves falling
and then the snow, and again
the small flowers rising up
out of dead leaves, the mosses
green again by the flowing water,
and the water thrush's nest
under the root of a strong tree.
I said, I will grieve no more
for death, for what is death to me
who have seen thy returns, O
Lord of love, who in the false are true.

VII

Those who give their thought
to seed, to love and the bringing to birth,
must know the sightless underside
of earth, and perhaps more than once,
for no one goes at no cost
to that place where what is dark,
more still than the hands
of the dead, remembers the light
again, and starts to move.

It is spring, and the little trees
that sprouted in the abandoned field
two years and more ago, striving
to grow, half-smothered under
the shadows of the tall weeds,
now rise above them
and spread their newleafed branches,
nothing between them and the light
sky, nothing at all.

VIII

I have again come home
through miles of sky
from hours of abstract talk
in the way of modern times
when humans live in their minds
and the world, forgotten, dies
into explanations. Weary
with absence, I return to earth.
"Good to see you back down
on the creek!" Martin Rowanberry
would say if he were here
to say it, as he'll not be again.
I have departed and returned
too many times to forget
that after all returns
one departure will remain.
I bring the horses down
off the hillside, harness them,
and start the morning's work,
the team quick to the load
along the narrow road.
I am weary with days
of travel, with poor sleep,
with time and error,
with every summer's heat
and blood-drinking flies.
And yet I sink into
the ancient happiness
of slow work in unhastenable
days and years. Horse and cow,

plow and hoe, grass to graze
and hay to mow have brought me
here, and taught me where I am.
I work in absence not yet mine
that will be mine. In time
this place has come to signify
the absence of many, and always
more, who once were here.
Day by day their voices
come to me, as from the air.
I remember them in what I do.
So I am not a modern man.
In my work I would be known
by forebears of a thousand years
if they were here to see it.
So it has been. So be it.

IX   Thirty-five Years

We have kept to the way we chose
in love without foresight
and long ago; it has come
to light only in the daylight
of each day as that day has come—
out of many possibilities, one:
an old house renewed upon its slope;
a long bringing in from garden,
field, and woods, not to be
hurried or increased beyond
the power of the place and day;
hope and grief freely given
to the unborn, the young, the old,
and the dead in their berths
under their silent names.
We have kept a daily faithfulness
to these, to one another, and to
this difficult, beautiful place,
arriving here again and again
out of distance, weariness,
or disappointment, to take it
by surprise, our surprise,
as the newborn take, after long
sightlessness, the light of day.
It is an old road that we
have followed, too narrow
to be traveled by more than two,
affording no place to turn
and go back, little improved
by the passage of forebears,

yet always renewed by growth
of the trees that lean over it,
by weather never two days the same,
and by our own delight
to see that it has led us
once again to an opening,
a small cultivated valley
among the wooded hills, familiar
as the oldest dream, where we know
we are, even as we do,
the work of love.

1993

I

No, no, there is no going back.
Less and less you are
that possibility you were.
More and more you have become
those lives and deaths
that have belonged to you.
You have become a sort of grave
containing much that was
and is no more in time, beloved
then, now, and always.
And so you have become a sort of tree
standing over a grave.
Now more than ever you can be
generous toward each day
that comes, young, to disappear
forever, and yet remain
unaging in the mind.
Every day you have less reason
not to give yourself away.

II

When my father was an old man,
past eighty years, we sat together
on the porch in silence
in the dark. Finally he said,
"Well, I have had a wonderful life,"
adding after a long pause,
"and I have had nothing
to do with it!" We were silent
for a while again. And then I asked,
"Well, do you believe in the
'informed decision'?" He thought
some more, and at last said
out of the darkness: "Naw!"
He was right, for when we choose
the way by which our only life
is lived, we choose and do not know
what we have chosen, for this
is the heart's choice, not the mind's;
to be true to the heart's one choice
is the long labor of the mind.
He chose, imperfectly as we must,
the rule of love, and learned
through years of light what darkly
he had chosen: his life, his place,
our place, our lives. And now comes
one he chose, but will not see:
Emily Rose, born May 2, 1993.

III

Now, surely, I am getting old,
for my memory of myself
as a young man seems now
to be complete, as a story told.
The young man leaps, and lands
on an old man's legs.

IV

Hate has no world.
The people of hate must try
to possess the world of love,
for it is the only world;
it is Heaven and Earth.
But as lonely, eager hate
possesses it, it disappears;
it never did exist,
and hate must seek another
world that love has made.

V   Remembering Evia

For Liadain, Denise, and Philip

We went in darkness where
We did not know, or why
Or how we'd come so far
Past sight or memory.

We climbed a narrow path
Up a moon-shadowed slope.
The guide we journeyed with
Held a small light. And step

By step our shadows rose
With us, and then fell back
Before the shine of windows
That opened in the black

Hillside, or so it seemed.
We reached a windy porch
As if both seen and dreamed
On its dark, lofty perch

Between the sky and sea.
A lamplit table spread
Old hospitality
Of cheese and wine and bread.

Darker than wine, the waves
Muttered upon the stones,
Asking whose time it was,
Our time or Agamemnon's.

The sea's undying sound
Demarked a land unknown
To us, who therein found
Welcome, our travel done.

1994

I

I leave the warmth of the stove,
my chair and book, and go out
into the cold night. My little lamp
that shows the way and leaves me dark
is swinging in my hand.
The house windows shine above me,
and below a single light gleams
in the barn where an hour ago
I left a ewe in labor. Beyond
is the grand sweep of Heaven's stars.
As I walk between them in the deep
night, the lights of house and barn
also are stars; my own small light
is an unsteady star.
I come to earth on the barn floor
where the ewe's lambs have been born
and now, wet and bloody, breathing
at last the air of this wintry world,
struggle to rise, while the ewe
mutters and licks. Unknowing,
they have the knack of their becoming:
heartbeat and breath,
the hunger that will lead them
to the tit, and thence to the sunlit
grass. I perform the ancient acts
of comfort and safety, making sure.
I linger a moment in the pleasure
of their coming and my welcome,
and then go, for I must comfort myself

and sleep. While I worked
the world turned half an hour,
carrying us on toward morning
and spring, the dark and the cold
again, the births and then the deaths
of many things, the end of time.
I close the door and walk back,
homeward, among the stars.

II

Finally will it not be enough,
after much living, after
much love, after much dying
of those you have loved,
to sit on the porch near sundown
with your eyes simply open,
watching the wind shape the clouds
into the shapes of clouds?

Even then you will remember
the history of love, shaped
in the shapes of flesh, everchanging
as the clouds that pass, the blessed
yearning of body for body,
unending light.
You will remember, watching
the clouds, the future of love.

III

(Ye must be born again.)

I think of Gloucester, blind, led through the world
To the world's edge by the hand of a stranger
Who is his faithful son. At the cliff's verge
He flings away his life, as of no worth,
The true way lost, his eyes two bleeding wounds—
And finds his life again, and is led on
By the forsaken son who has become
His father, that the good may recognize
Each other, and at last go ripe to death.
We live the given life, and not the planned.

IV

They sit together on the porch, the dark
Almost fallen, the house behind them dark.
Their supper done with, they have washed and dried
The dishes—only two plates now, two glasses,
Two knives, two forks, two spoons—small work for two.
She sits with her hands folded in her lap,
At rest. He smokes his pipe. They do not speak.
And when they speak at last it is to say
What each one knows the other knows. They have
One mind between them, now, that finally
For all its knowing will not exactly know
Which one goes first through the dark doorway, bidding
Goodnight, and which sits on a while alone.

V

For Maxine Kumin

Raking hay on a rough slope,
when I was about sixteen,
I drove to the ridgetop and saw
in a neighbor's field on the other side
a pond in a swale, and around it
the whole field filled
with chicory in bloom, blue
as the sky reflected in the pond—
bluer even, and somehow lighter,
though they belonged to gravity.
They were the morning's
blossoms and would not last.
But I go back now in my mind
to when I drew the long windrow
to the top of the rise, and I see
the blue-flowered field, holding
in its center the sky-reflecting pond.
It seems, as then, another world
in this world, such as a pilgrim
might travel days and years
to find, and find at last
on the morning of his return
by his mere being at home
awake—a moment seen, forever known.

VI

A man is lying on a bed
in a small room in the dark.
Weary and afraid, he prays
for courage to sleep, to wake
and work again; he doubts
that waking when he wakes
will recompense his sleep.
His prayers lean upward
on the dark and fall
like flares from a catastrophe.
He is a man breathing the fear
of hopeless prayer, prayed
in hope. He breathes the prayer
of his fear that gives a light
by which he sees only himself lying
in the dark, a low mound asking
almost nothing at all.
And then, long yet before dawn,
comes what he had not thought:
love that causes him to stir
like the dead in the grave, being
remembered—his own love or
Heaven's, he does not know.
But now it is all around him;
it comes down upon him
like a summer rain falling
slowly, quietly in the dark.

VII

I would not have been a poet
except that I have been in love
alive in this mortal world,
or an essayist except that I
have been bewildered and afraid,
or a storyteller had I not heard
stories passing to me through the air,
or a writer at all except
I have been wakeful at night
and words have come to me
out of their deep caves
needing to be remembered.
But on the days I am lucky
or blessed, I am silent.
I go into the one body
that two make in making marriage
that for all our trying, all
our deaf-and-dumb of speech,
has no tongue. Or I give myself
to gravity, light, and air
and am carried back
to solitary work in fields
and woods, where my hands
rest upon a world unnamed,
complete, unanswerable, and final
as our daily bread and meat.
The way of love leads all ways
to life beyond words, silent
and secret. To serve that triumph
I have done all the rest.

VIII

And now this leaf lies brightly on the ground.

1995

I

A man with some authentic worries
And many vain and silly ones,
I am well-schooled in sleeplessness;
I know it from the inside out.
I breathe, and I know what's at stake.

But still sometimes I'm sane and sound,
However heart or head may ache;
I go to sleep when I lie down.
With no determined care to breathe,
I breathe and live and sleep and take

A sabbath from my weariness.
I rest in an unasking trust
Like clouds and ponds and stones and trees.
The long-arising Day will break
If I should die before I wake.

II

The best reward in going to the woods
Is being lost to other people, and
Lost sometimes to myself. I'm at the end
Of no bespeaking wire to spoil my goods;

I send no letter back I do not bring.
Whoever wants me now must hunt me down
Like something wild, and wild is anything
Beyond the reach of purpose not its own.

Wild is anything that's not at home
In something else's place. This good white oak
Is not an orchard tree, is unbespoke,
And it can live here by its will alone,

Lost to all other wills but Heaven's—wild.
So where I most am found I'm lost to you,
Presuming friend, and only can be called
Or answered by a certain one, or two.

III   A Brass Bowl

Worn to brightness, this
bowl opens outward
to the world, like
the marriage of a pair
we sometimes know.
Filled full, it holds
not greedily. Empty,
it fills with light
that is Heaven's and
its own. It holds
forever for a while.

IV   Amish Economy

We live by mercy if we live.
To that we have no fit reply
But working well and giving thanks,
Loving God, loving one another,
To keep Creation's neighborhood.

And my friend David Kline told me,
"It falls strangely on Amish ears,
This talk of how you find yourself.
We Amish, after all, don't try
To find ourselves. We try to lose
Ourselves"—and thus are lost within
The found world of sunlight and rain
Where fields are green and then are ripe,
And the people eat together by
The charity of God, who is kind
Even to those who give no thanks.

In morning light, men in dark clothes
Go out among the beasts and fields.
Lest the community be lost,
Each day they must work out the bond
Between goods and their price: the garden
Weeded by sweat is flowerbright;
The wheat shocked in shorn fields, clover
Is growing where wheat grew; the crib
Is golden with the gathered corn,

While in the world of the found selves,
Lost to the sunlit, rainy world,
The motor-driven cannot stop.

This is the world where value is
Abstract, and preys on things, and things
Are changed to thoughts that have a price.
Cost + greed – fear = price:
Maury Telleen thus laid it out.
The need to balance greed and fear
Affords no stopping place, no rest,
And need increases as we fail.

But now, in summer dusk, a man
Whose hair and beard curl like spring ferns
Sits under the yard trees, at rest,
His smallest daughter on his lap.
This is because he rose at dawn,
Cared for his own, helped his neighbors,
Worked much, spent little, kept his peace.

V

*To my granddaughters who visited the Holocaust
Museum on the day of the burial of Yitzhak Rabin*

Now you know the worst
we humans have to know
about ourselves, and I am sorry,

for I know that you will be afraid.
To those of our bodies given
without pity to be burned, I know

there is no answer
but loving one another,
even our enemies, and this is hard.

But remember:
when a man of war becomes a man of peace,
he gives a light, divine

though it is also human.
When a man of peace is killed
by a man of war, he gives a light.

You do not have to walk in darkness.
If you will have the courage for love,
you may walk in light. It will be

the light of those who have suffered
for peace. It will be
your light.

VI   The Old Man Climbs a Tree

He had a tall cedar he wanted to cut for posts,
but it leaned backward toward the fence,
and there's no gain in tearing down one
fence to build another. To preserve the fence
already built, he needed to fasten a rope
high up in the cedar, and draw it tight
to the trunk of another tree, so that as he sawed
the cedar free of its stance it would sway
away from the fence as it fell. To bring
a ladder would require too long a carry
up through the woods. Besides, you can't
climb into a cedar tree by means of a ladder—
too bristly. He would need first to cut off
all the branches, and for that would need a ladder.

And so, he thought, he would need to climb
the tree itself. He'd climbed trees many times
in play when he was a boy, and many times
since, when he'd had a reason. He'd loved
always his reasons for climbing trees.
But he'd come now to the age of remembering,
and he remembered his boyhood fall from an apple tree,
and being brought in to his mother, his wits
dispersed, not knowing where he was,
though where he was was this world still.
If that should happen now, he thought,
the world he waked up in would not be this one.
The other world is nearer to him now.
But trailing his rope untied as yet to anything
but himself, he climbed up once again and stood
where only birds and the wind had been before,

and knew it was another world, after all,
that he had climbed up into. There are
no worlds but other worlds: the world
of the field mouse, the world of the hawk,
the world of the beetle, the world of the oak,
the worlds of the unborn, the dead, and all
the heavenly host, and he is alive
in those worlds while living in his own.
Known or unknown, every world exists
because the others do.

              The treetops
are another world, smelling of bark,
a stratum of freer air and larger views,
from which he saw the world he'd lived in
all day until now, its intimate geography changed
by his absence and by the height he saw it from.
The sky was a little larger, and all around
the aerial topography of treetops, green and gray,
the ground almost invisible beneath.
He perched there, ungravitied as a bird,
knotting his rope and looking about, worlded
in worlds on worlds, pleased, and unafraid.

There are no worlds but other worlds
and all the other worlds are here,
reached or almost reachable by the same
outstretching hand, as he, perched upon
his high branch, almost imagined flight.
And yet when he descended into this other
other world, he climbed down all the way.
He did not swing out from a lower limb
and drop, as once he would have done.

1996

I

Now you have slipped away
Under the trackless snow,
To you the time of day
Always is long ago.

You're safe among the dead,
Alive, your death undone.
"Come and dine," Christ said.
Consenting, you have gone.

II

On summer evenings we sat in the yard,
the house dark, the stars bright overhead.
The laps and arms of the old
held the young. As we talked we knew
by the dark distances of Heaven's lights
our smallness, and the greatness of our love.

Now from that upland once surrounded
by the horizon of unbroken dark, we
(who were children only a life ago)
see reflected on the clouds the lights
of three cities, as if we offer to the sky
some truth of ours that we are certain of,

or as if we will have no light
but our own, and thus make illusory
all the light we have.

III

It is almost spring again.
At the woods' edge the redbird
sings his happiest note: sweet,
sweet, sweet, sweet. And you,
who have left this world forever,
have been gone one day.

March 15, 1996

IV

A long time ago, returning
from a trip to see a girl
with whom I was in love,
I stopped on the roadside
above this house where I now live.
I had driven all day and on
into the night. Now it was late.
Moonlight covered the world,
and the valley was filled
with voices, the whippoorwills
calling and answering
in the hollows and along the slopes,
so that their music seemed
to gather and flow as the moonlight
flowed and touched lightly
every upward leaf and grassblade.
I stood still a long time for fear
that any sound I made
would cause that flood of light,
which was singing which was
light, to flow away forever
from this flawed world. I forgot
the misery of a boy's love
inevitably selfish, and a selfless
happiness freely came to me
from this place, to which my heart
also had been given.

V

Some Sunday afternoon, it may be,
you are sitting under your porch roof,
looking down through the trees
to the river, watching the rain. The circles
made by the raindrops' striking
expand, intersect, dissolve,

and suddenly (for you are getting on
now, and much of your life is memory)
the hands of the dead, who have been here
with you, rest upon you tenderly
as the rain rests shining
upon the leaves. And you think then

(for thought will come) of the strangeness
of the thought of Heaven, for now
you have imagined yourself there,
remembering with longing this
happiness, this rain. Sometimes here
we are there, and there is no death.

VI

A bird the size
of a leaf fills
the whole lucid
evening with
his note, and flies.

VII

In spring we planted seed,
And by degrees the plants
Grew, flowered, and transformed
The light to food, which we
Brought in, and ate, and lived.
The year grown old, we gathered
All that remained. We broke,
Manured, prepared the ground
For overwintering,
And thus at last made clear
Our little plot of time,
Tropical for a while,
Then temperate, then cold.

VIII

Our Christmas tree is
not electrified, is not
covered with little lights
calling attention to themselves
(we have had enough
of little lights calling attention
to themselves). Our tree
is a cedar cut here, one
of the fragrances of our place,
hung with painted cones
and paper stars folded
long ago to praise our tree,
Christ come into the world.

1997

I

Best of any song
is bird song
in the quiet, but first
you must have the quiet.

II

Even while I dreamed I prayed that what I saw was only fear
     and no foretelling,
for I saw the last known landscape destroyed for the sake
of the objective, the soil bulldozed, the rock blasted.
Those who had wanted to go home would never get there
     now.

I visited the offices where for the sake of the objective the
     planners planned
at blank desks set in rows. I visited the loud factories
where the machines were made that would drive ever
     forward
toward the objective. I saw the forest reduced to stumps and
     gullies; I saw
the poisoned river, the mountain cast into the valley;
I came to the city that nobody recognized because it looked
     like every other city.
I saw the passages worn by the unnumbered
footfalls of those whose eyes were fixed upon the objective.

Their passing had obliterated the graves and the
     monuments
of those who had died in pursuit of the objective
and who had long ago forever been forgotten, according
to the inevitable rule that those who have forgotten forget
that they have forgotten. Men, women, and children now
     pursued the objective
as if nobody ever had pursued it before.

The races and the sexes now intermingled perfectly in
     pursuit of the objective.

The once-enslaved, the once-oppressed were now free
to sell themselves to the highest bidder
and to enter the best-paying prisons
in pursuit of the objective, which was the destruction of all
enemies,
which was the destruction of all obstacles, which was the
destruction of all objects,
which was to clear the way to victory, which was to clear the
way to promotion, to salvation, to progress,
to the completed sale, to the signature
on the contract, which was to clear the way
to self-realization, to self-creation, from which nobody who
ever wanted to go home
would ever get there now, for every remembered place
had been displaced; the signposts had been bent to the
ground and covered over.

Every place had been displaced, every love
unloved, every vow unsworn, every word unmeant
to make way for the passage of the crowd
of the individuated, the autonomous, the self-actuated,
the homeless
with their many eyes opened only toward the objective
which they did not yet perceive in the far distance,
having never known where they were going,
having never known where they came from.

III

I was wakened from my dream of the ruined world by the
    sound
of rain falling slowly onto the dry earth of my place in time.
On the parched garden, the cracked-open pastures,
the dusty grape leaves, the brittled grass, the drooping
    foliage of the woods,
fell still the quiet rain.

IV

"You see," my mother said, and laughed,
knowing I knew the passage
she was remembering, "finally you lose
everything." She had lost
parents, husband, and friends, youth,
health, most comforts, many hopes.

Deaf, asleep in her chair, awakened
by a hand's touch, she would look up
and smile in welcome as quiet
as if she had seen us coming.

She watched, curious and affectionate,
the sparrows, titmice, and chickadees
she fed at her kitchen window—
where did they come from, where
did they go? No matter.
They came and went as freely as
in the time of her old age
her children came and went,
uncaptured, but fed.

And I, walking in the first spring
of her absence, know again
her inextinguishable delight:
the wild bluebells, the yellow
celandine, violets purple
and white, twinleaf, bloodroot,
larkspur, the rue anemone
light, light under the big trees,

and overhead the redbud blooming,
the redbird singing,
the oak leaves like flowers still
unfolding, and the blue sky.

V

The lovers know the loveliness
That is not of their bodies only
(Though they be lovely) but is of
Their bodies given up to love.

They find the open-heartedness
Of two desires which both are lonely
Until by dying they have their living,
And gain all they have lost in giving,

Each offering the desired desire.
Beyond what time requires, they are
What they surpass themselves to make;
They give the pleasure that they take.

VI

Now, as a man learning
the limits of time, I look anew
at a familiar carving: a ring
of granite drawing to a circle

all space around it, and enclosing
a circle. In cross section, the stone
itself is square. It doubles
the superficial strip of Möbius

and thus makes of two surfaces
a solid, dimensioned
as the body, a pure thought
shaped in stone. One surface

is rough, the other smooth,
to invite hand or eye into
its windings, to remind the mind
in its travels, the long and far

of its restless reckoning,
that where it comes from
and where it is going
are nowhere in the distance,

not in the future or the past,
but are forever here
now. The stone turns
without limit within itself,

dark within light, light
within dark. What is above
descends, what is below rises.
So the carver wrought it out

until it came to rest.
So what is inward turns outward
as does, we are told, the Kingdom of God.
So we contain that which contains us.

So the departed come to light.

VII

There is a day
when the road neither
comes nor goes, and the way
is not a way but a place.